# My dog likes me

## Bobbie Kalman

🍄 **Crabtree Publishing Company**

www.crabtreebooks.com

# Created by Bobbie Kalman

**Author and
Editor-in-Chief**
Bobbie Kalman

**Reading consultant**
Elaine Hurst

**Editors**
Kathy Middleton
Crystal Sikkens

**Photo research**
Bobbie Kalman

**Design**
Bobbie Kalman
Katherine Berti

**Production coordinator
and Prepress technician**
Katherine Berti

**Photographs**
Marc Crabtree: page 15 (bottom left)
Other photographs by Shutterstock

**Library and Archives Canada Cataloguing in Publication**

Kalman, Bobbie, 1947-
    My dog likes me / Bobbie Kalman.

(My world)
ISBN 978-0-7787-9499-8 (bound).--ISBN 978-0-7787-9524-7 (pbk.)

    1. Dogs--Juvenile literature. 2. Children and animals--Juvenile
literature. 3. Human-animal relationships--Juvenile literature.
I. Title. II. Series: My world (St. Catharines, Ont.)

SF426.5.K34 2011          j636.7          C2010-901968-7

**Library of Congress Cataloging-in-Publication Data**

Kalman, Bobbie.
  My dog likes me / Bobbie Kalman.
      p. cm. -- (My world)
  ISBN 978-0-7787-9524-7 (pbk. : alk. paper) -- ISBN 978-0-7787-9499-8
(reinforced library binding : alk. paper)
  1. Dogs--Juvenile literature. 2. Children and animals--Juvenile
literature. 3. Human-animal relationships--Juvenile literature. I. Title.
II. Series.

  SF426.5.K359 2011
  636.7--dc22

                                                    2010011294

## Crabtree Publishing Company

Printed in China/072010/AP20100226

www.crabtreebooks.com        1-800-387-7650

**Published in Canada
Crabtree Publishing**
616 Welland Ave.
St. Catharines, Ontario
L2M 5V6

**Published in the United States
Crabtree Publishing**
PMB 59051
350 Fifth Avenue, 59th Floor
New York, New York 10118

**Published in the United Kingdom
Crabtree Publishing**
Maritime House
Basin Road North, Hove
BN41 1WR

**Published in Australia
Crabtree Publishing**
386 Mt. Alexander Rd.
Ascot Vale (Melbourne)
VIC 3032

cr 1/11/11  02-63960

# Words to know

bath

dancing

fish

hugging

jumping

learning
(teaching)

leaves
(playing)

looking (water)

singing

walking

3

I like my dog.

I like hugging my dog.

My dog likes me.

My dog likes hugging me.

My dog likes looking at fish jump.

My dog likes jumping like the fish.

My dog likes playing in water.

My dog likes playing in leaves.

My dog likes singing.

My dog likes dancing.

I am teaching my dog to sit.
My dog likes learning.

Do you like giving your dog a bath?
Do you like walking your dog?

# Notes for adults

## Objectives
- to allow children to share their experiences with dogs
- to allow children to learn verbs in the present continuous tense, ending in "ing"
- to learn about dog behavior and interaction with pet dogs

## Before reading the book
Write these frequently used words on the board: my, dog, likes
Ask these questions:
"Do you have a dog?"
"What are some things that all dogs do?" (walk, run, sit, talk, bark)
"What things does your dog, or a dog you know, do?"

## Questions after reading the book
"How do you show that you like your dog?"
"How does your dog show that it likes you?"
"What are some of the things the dogs in the book like to do?" (looking, jumping, hugging, playing, singing, dancing, bathing, walking, learning)

## Activity: Dog bookmark
Ask the children to cut out small pictures of dogs from magazines or have them draw and color their own pictures. Cut strips of cardboard or stiff paper and glue the dog pictures onto the strips. Have the children exchange their dog "bookmarks" with their friends.

## Looking after a dog
Ask the children to draw pictures of all the ways they need to care for a dog: walking the dog, bathing it, feeding it, brushing its coat, etc.

## Ending in "ing"
Ask the children to say these words with "ing" endings: hug, look, jump, play, sing, dance, teach, learn, give, walk.

## Extension
Read **Wild and Pet Puppies** to the children. Acquaint them with the other animals that belong to the "dog family." How are wild dogs and pet dogs different?

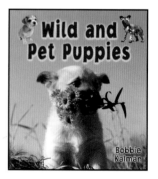

This book is part of the *It's fun to learn about baby animals* series.
*Guided Reading: J*

*For teacher's guide, go to www.crabtreebooks.com/teachersguides*